Tic-Tac-Toe for the HP 35s Scientific Calculator

– what tic-tac-toe can demonstrate

about game programming –

By Frederick S. Ruland

Dedicated to All at Instytut Zootechniki in Kraków

Contents:

Introduction:

The goal of this little book is to demonstrate a few features of the HP 35s, and share some programming hints and simulation techniques relative to games. While the focus is on the HP 35s, many of the concepts discussed can be used with most programmable calculators.

Although Tic-Tac-Toe is used as an example, most of the concepts discussed are generic in nature and could be used in a variety of games.

Equally important to the programming approaches are the techniques for monitoring the moves of multiple players, and the strategy for offensive and defense play.

The HP 35s has 801 indirect storage registers and 26 direct storage registers. This book demonstrates the 'indexed' approach to accessing both types of registers. The HP 35s can store at least 26 programs subject to the 30K storage limitation for programs and data.

Although the HP 35s lacks a computer interface and a graphics display, it is reasonably priced at about $55 (July 2020). One of the attractions of the HP 35s is its ability to use Reverse Polish Notation (RPN).

The target audience for this book is the casual or infrequent HP 35s user wishing to expand their knowledge and use of the calculator – however, the book assumes no prior HP 35s experience. Explanations are provided for each command, along with the key locations – of which there are roughly 150 on the keypad.

I hope the reader will find this book useful, and also have a bit of fun playing the game.

Note: This book does not cover every aspect of the HP 35s. Therefore it is important to have the HP 35s User's Guide which is available free online.

http://support.hp.com/us-en/product/hp-35s-scientific-calculator/3442983/manuals

Overview:

The Tic-Tac-Toe game consists of five 'linked' programs. Each focuses on certain components of the game, for example: keeping track of moves by different players; checking to make sure cells are not occupied before making automated moves; and checking a 'strategy table' for where and when to make offensive and defensive moves.

The two 'opponents' will be referred to as the 'player' and the 'computer'. The moves by the computer are initially made at random based on cell importance (i.e., center and corners being considered more important). However, when two cells in any one of eight 'win paths' are both occupied by either the player, or by the computer, the strategy table then controls the computer's moves. In any case, after moves by either the player or the computer, the strategy table is updated.

Since the HP 35s has only two lines of display, it was decided to have the player keep track of the moves and determine when a win occurs.

If one is simply interested in playing the game, they might enter the five programs, try out the game, and return later for any supporting material.

,,,,,,,,,,,,,,,,,,,

The Programs:

Each program is discussed in its own section. However they are introduced below, in brief, to show where each fits into the overall scheme of things.

Each program performs from one to four tasks and then hands off control to the next program.

Program A could be considered the main program with B, D, E, and V acting as 'subroutines'. Program A performs initial 'housekeep' tasks, and determines/monitors whose move takes place.

Program B is called only once to store frequency information for the random moves made by Program E.

Program D defines the eight winning paths and updates the strategy table after each move.

Program E generates cell moves at random if no win/block moves are deemed necessary by Program V.

Program V queries the strategy table and executes either an automated win/block move, or calls for a random move.

As an Aside: The programs, in total, consist of 445 statements. Most statements include comments inside brackets '[ ]' and detailed explanations following each program.

Note: Appendix L contains details on the HP 35s subroutine capabilities.

,,,,,,,,,,,,,,,,,,,,

Entering and Storing a Program – Quick Review:

If you are new to the HP 35s, or haven't used your calculator for some time, the following tiny example may serve as a guide for entering and running a program.

On and OFF:

Pressing C [bottom left corner] or BLUE then C [both in bottom left corner] will turn the calculator on. YELLOW then C will turn it off.

In that we will use RPN throughout, you can switch to this mode by pressing MODE [top right] and then option 5 for RPN.

Let's say you want to enter and save a program called 'Z', but don't recall if you already have a program by that name. You can check the memory area for program labels as follows:

YELLOW [bottom left] **MEM** [top right] then **2** [to select the PGM option] then use the arrows ^ v [top right] to scroll.

If you see something like the following, you already have a program Z:

LBL Z

LN = 62

If you would like to delete this program, press BLUE CLEAR while LBL Z is displayed.

Press **C** [bottom left corner] to escape the menu.

Comment: You can check Appendix B for additional Program/Memory Management details.

We are ready now to enter our test program. The material inside brackets [ ] is explanatory and is not entered.

GTO . . [GTO followed by two decimal points, to set the programming pointer to the top of the program storage area]

BLUE PRGM [to shift to programming mode – you will see PRGM TOP]

BLUE LBL Z [you will see Z001 LBL Z – the line numbers are added automatically with Z as the prefix]

YELLOW INPUT A   [will request a value for A when you execute the program]

YELLOW INPUT B   [will request a value for B]

+   [plus sign adds A and B]

BLUE STO C   [stores sum as C]

YELLOW VIEW C   [displays C]

YELLOW RTN   [RTN = return and marks the end of program]

Press **C** to exit programming mode   [when you exit, the program is saved]

Now to Run/Execute the Program:

XEQ Z ENTER

You will be asked for A?

For example, enter **3** then press **R/S**   [R/S = Run/Stop]

You will be asked for B?

Enter **5** then press **R/S**

You will see C = 8 [then press **R/S**]

You will now be back at the 'default' numerical display.

,,,,,,,,,,,,,,,,,,,,

Returning to Tic-Tac-Toe:

Program A:

Program A acts as the main program. It performs 'housekeeping' chores, monitors whose turn it is, records the player's move, and calls other programs to evaluate and decide on the computer's move. Housekeeping chores include, among other things, controlling the display format, initialization of variables, and the setting of 'flags'.   Additional statement details are given inside brackets [ ] and in comments following the program.

Entering Program A:

GTO ..   [sets program pointer]

BLUE PRGM   [shifts to programming mode]

A001 BLUE LBL A   [Main Calling Program]

A002 YELLOW DISPLAY [option **1** then **0** when you see FIX __ Will show as **FIX 0**]

[Drops digits after the decimal point for easier reading of moves]

A003 BLUE CLEAR [option 2 VARS, clears variables A to Z, shows as **CLVARS**]

A004 YELLOW FLAGS [option **2**, then **decimal point**, then **0**, shows as **CF 10**]

[Clears flag 10 for program D to evaluate 'equations']

A005 XEQ B001   [the random choices array setup]

A006 YELLOW INPUT W [Whose turn? W for Who plays? 0=program, 1=player]

A007 BLUE X?0 [option **6**, shows as **X=0?**]

A008 XEQ V001 [true, i.e., W = 0 and program plays]

[if 0 was entered, goes to V001. If 1 entered, goes to INPUT]

A009 YELLOW INPUT M   [M for player's move, 1 to 9]

A010 +/ − [now minus 1 to minus 9] [the **+/- key** and not three separate symbols]

A011 BLUE STO J   [1 to 9 is now − 1 to − 9 to indicate variables A to I]

A012 1   [plus 1, player's occupied code]

A013 BLUE STO (J)

A014 YELLOW VIEW M   [1 to 9]

A015 XEQ D001 [update strategy table]

A016 YELLOW RTN

Press **C** to escape programming mode.

Note: See Appendix B regarding the following program storage details:

LBL A   [program label/name]

LN = 62   [program length in bytes]

CK = 5711   [program checksum − a unique hexadecimal code]

,,,,,,,,,,,,,,,,,,,,,,

Program A Explanations by Statement Number:

A002: Sets the display for 0 digits to the right of the decimal point.

A003: Clears direct variables (A through Z) before each run.

A004: Clears FLAG 10 to ensure that program D will process equations.

A005: Calls program B to assign values to the random choice area. Program B returns to A006.

A006: W? is the prompt for 'Who Plays.' The player = 1, the computer = 0.

A008: Calls program V when it is the computer's turn to make a move.

A009: M? Prompts for the player's Move. Player enters 1 through 9.

A010 – A011: The cell number chosen is changed to a negative value to access the nine direct access variables A through I via (J) indexing.

A012: To indicate that the player occupies the cell, a 1 is used. Note: Cells occupied by the computer are set to minus 1 in Program V.

A014: Displays the move with 'M ='(the move made, in this case, by the player).

A015: Calls program D to update the game's strategy table with this most recent move.

Note: For additional program entry and editing information, see Appendix C.

,,,,,,,,,,,,,,,,,,,,,,

Program B:

Program B sets up the random choice area for use when neither a 'block' nor a 'win' is eminent based on the strategy table.

Program B stores cell values 1 to 9 (multiple times) in indirect storage locations 1 to 16 depending upon the importance of the cell location (corners and center having higher presumed value). See table below.

Nonzero value (e.g., 999) is first stored in location 17 to ensure access to the indirect storage locations 1 to 16. While this is always a good practice, in this instance it is not absolutely necessary, in that we are initially storing data as opposed to recalling data).

Note: Program B is only called once and is the only 'subroutine' which returns to Program A (at A006) in true subroutine fashion.

Cell Number and Frequencies for the 16 Random Chance Moves Area

Cell	Frequency	Location
1	2	corner
2	1	
3	2	corner
4	1	
5	4	center
6	1	
7	2	corner
8	1	
9	2	corner

,,,,,,,,,,,,,,,,,,,,,

Comment: Just a few words regarding indirect variables: There are 801 indirect variables. These indirect variables are accessed via the functions (I) and (J). For example, to store a value, say 777, in the third indirect variable, one would do the following if choosing to use (J):

3

BLUE STO J   [J is set to 3]

777

BLUE STO (J)   [the third indirect variable is set to 777]

Note: For additional information regarding Indirect variables see Appendix D.

Entering Program B:

GTO . .

BLUE PRGM

B001 BLUE LBL B

B002 17

B003 BLUE STO J   [J will be the index value for the (J) function below]

B004 999

B005 BLUE STO (J) [999 will be stored as indirect variable 17]

[statements B001 to B005 enable access to the indirect variables 1 to 16]

[the corner cells (1, 3, 7, 9) are weighted by 2 (repeated twice), and the center (5) is weighted by 4 relative to the off-corners (2, 4, 6, 8)]

B006 1   [cell location 1 of 16]

B007 BLUE STO J

B008 1   [value 1 saved in above location]

B009 BLUE STO (J)

B010 2   [cell location 2 of 16]

B011 BLUE STO J

B012 1   [value 1 saved in above location]

B013 BLUE STO (J)

B014 3   [cell location 3 of 16]

B015 BLUE STO J

B016 3   [value 3 saved in above location]

B017 BLUE STO (J)

B018 4   [cell location 4 of 16]

B019 BLUE STO J

B020 3   [value 3 saved in above location]

BLUE 21 BLUE STO (J)

B022 5   [cell location 5 of 16]

B023 BLUE STO J

B024 7   [value 7 saved in above location]

B025 BLUE STO (J)

B026 6   [cell location 6 of 16]

B027 BLUE STO J

B028 7   [value 7 saved in above location]

B029 BLUE STO (J)

B030 7   [cell location 7 of 16]

B031 BLUE STO J

B032 9   [value 9 saved in above location]

B033 BLUE STO (J)

B034 8   [cell location 8 of 16]

B035 BLUE STO J

B036 9   [value 9 saved in above location]

B037 BLUE STO (J)

B038 9   [cell location 9 of 16]

B039 BLUE STO J

B040 5   [value 5 saved in above location]

B041 BLUE STO (J)

B042 10   [cell location 10 of 16]

B043 BLUE STO J

B044 5   [value 5 saved in above location]

B045 BLUE STO (J)

B046 11   [cell location 11 of 16]

B047 BLUE STO J

B048 2   [value 2 saved in above location]

B049 BLUE STO (J)

B050 12   [cell location 12 of 16]

B051 BLUE STO J

B052 4   [value 4 saved in above location]

B053 BLUE STO (J)

B054 13   [cell location 13 of 16]

B055 BLUE STO J

B056 5   [value 5 saved in above location]

B057 BLUE STO (J)

B058 14   [cell location 14 of 16]

B059 BLUE STO J

B060 6   [value 6 saved in above location]

B061 BLUE STO (J)

B062 15   [cell location 15 of 16]

B063 BLUE STO J

B064 8   [value 8 saved in above location]

B065 BLUE STO (J)

B066 16   [cell location 16 of 16]

B067 BLUE STO J

B068 5   [value 5 saved in above location]

B069 BLUE STO (J)

B070 YELLOW RTN

Press **C** to escape programming mode.

LBL B

LN = 254

CK = 0A02

Program B Explanations by Statement Number:

B002 – B005: Puts 999 in the indirect storage position 17. This location is just beyond locations 1 to 16 that we need to use. Technically, since we are initially <u>storing</u> – as opposed to <u>recalling</u> – this prior initialization could be omitted. However, this is a good, safe programming practice.

B006 – B007: Stores the indirect storage location (1 to 16) in variable J to use as the index for the function (J) in statement B009.

B008 – B009: Stores the cell number (1 to 9) in the location specified by B006 – B007 above, using the (J) indexing function.

Note: The above repeats for the 16 storage locations used for the random choice moves.

,,,,,,,,,,,,,,,,,,,,,

Program D:

Program D is the data collection area for the game's 'strategy table'.

Program D is called by Program A after the player's move, and called by program V after the computer's move in order to update the 8 paths [shown next] of the strategy table.

An Example of Updating the Strategy Table:

The player's moves (see below) are indicated by a 1 and the computer's moves are indicated by a − 1 (negative 1).

Let's say the player moves first to cell 3.

The computer then moves to cell 5.

The player then moves to cell 1.

Cell Number (computer)	with codes 1 (player) and -1
1 2 3	1 0 1 [winning path K = A + B + C = 2]
4 5 6	0 -1 0
7 8 9	0 0 0

Program D would compute path K as 1 + 0 + 1 = 2.

Program V (discussed below) finding K = 2, would initiate the computer's move to cell 2 (i.e., variable B) to block.

Note: See also Appendix S for more strategy table details.

,,,,,,,,,,,,,,,,,,,,

Eight Winning Paths: [Note the variables associated with each cell and its sum.]

Cell	Variables Sum	
1 2 3	(A B C) = K	
4 5 6	(D E F) = L	
7 8 9	(G H I) = N	[Note: M was used elsewhere]
1 4 7	(A D G) = O	
2 5 8	(B E H) = P	

3 6 9   (C F I) = Q

1 5 9   (A E I) = R

3 5 7   (C E G) = S

Note: Program V [next to be discussed] searches these paths in the order listed, which one might desire to change.

,,,,,,,,,,,,,,,,,,,,

Note Regarding the EQN Statements:

When pressing the EQN key, the EQN will not show. RCL must be pressed before the variable letters, A, B, C, etc. EQN statements function in algebraic mode.

Entering Program D:

GTO . .

BLUE PRGM

D001 BLUE LBL D

D002 EQN A + B + C STO K   [EQN RCL A + RCL B + RCL C BLUE STO K]

[BLUE STO will appear as a little triangle pointer]

D003 EQN D + E + F STO L

D004 EQN G + H + I STO N [Note: Variable M is used elsewhere]

D005 EQN A + D + G STO O

D006 EQN B + E + H STO P

D007 EQN C + F + I STO Q

D008 EQN A + E + I STO R

D009 EQN C + E + G STO S

D010 GTO A006 [i.e., who plays in Program A – INPUT W]

D011 YELLOW RTN

Press **C** to escape programming mode.

LBL D

LN = 89

CK = 7FD0

Note: There is a second version of Program D in Appendix Q which includes eight VIEW statements (one for each path) in case you want to monitor the workings of the strategy table.

Note: The EQN statements [D002 – D009] are processed in algebraic mode (and FLAG 10 must be cleared). This is the one exception to this book's total use of RPN.

The use of this single algebraic statement (per path) replaces 6 RPN statements:

For Example:

EQN A + B + C STO K would require 6 RPN statements as follows:

RCL A

RCL B

+

RCL C

+

STO K

Program V:

If Program D is the data collection area for the game's 'strategy table', then program V is the decision making area which uses the 'strategy table'.

Program V queries the sums of the 8 winning paths (i.e., variables K through S, excluding M). If the sum of the path is 2, the player is threating; or if minus 2, the computer has a winning chance.

The computer checks the three cells in the path. If a cell is zero (i.e., missing), it is replaced with minus 1 to either block or win. Program D is then called to update the strategy table. If no path needs attention, Program E is called to select an unoccupied cell at random (accordion to the frequencies).

Note: If the player (coded as 1) and the computer (coded as -1) each occupy a cell in the path, the path total is zero. When the computer selects a cell, a minus 1 is inserted after checking that the cell is unoccupied.

Entering Program V:

GTO . .

BLUE PRGM

V001 LBL V

V002 RCL K   [A B C = K path]

V003 BLUE ABS [absolute value, looking for 2 or – 2]

V004 2

V005 –

V006 BLUE X?0 [option **6**, shows as **X=0?**] [will = 0 if (1 & 1) or (-1 & -1)]

V007 GTO V009   [need to block/win]

V008 GTO V040   [go to next path L at V040]

V009 RCL A [will be 0, 1 or – 1]

V010 BLUE X?0 [option **1**, shows as **X not =0?**]

V011 GTO V019 [if true that A not = 0, i.e., cell 1 was already chosen]

12 1   [therefore A = 0] [Note: Press 1 then ENTER]

13 +/-   [– 1 represents the computer]

14 BLUE STO A   [stores – 1 in A]

15 1   [1 because A represents cell 1]

V016 BLUE STO M

V017 YELLOW VIEW M

V018 XEQ D001   [update 'K tables' then to who plays]

,,,,,,,,,,,,,,,,,,,,,,

V019 RCL B

V020 BLUE X?0 [option **1**, shows as **X not =0?**]

V021 GTO V029 [i.e., B not = 0]

V022 1 [therefore B = 0] [Note: Press 1 then ENTER]

V023 +/- [− 1 represents the computer]

V024 BLUE STO B

V025 2   [2 because B represents cell 2]

V026 BLUE STO M

V027 YELLOW VIEW M

V028 XEQ D001 [update 'K tables' then to who plays]

,,,,,,,,,,,,,,,,,,,,

V029 RCL C

V030 BLUE X?0 [option **1** shows a X not =0?]

V031 GTO V039 [C not = 0] [If program (line 8) works properly, program should not go here]

V032 1 [C = 0] [Note: Press 1 then ENTER]

V033 +/- [− 1 represents the computer]

V034 BLUE STO C

V035 3 [3 because C represents cell 3]

V036 BLUE STO M

V037 YELOW VIEW M

V038 XEQ D001 [update 'K tables' then to who plays]

V039 XEQ E001 [go to random move]

Explanation for line V039: In essence, program should not go here at this stage. If it does, it means that K equaled 2 (or minus 2), but the 'missing' cell was not missing. (I admit, I added this statement out of an abundance of caution.)

////////////////

V040 RCL L [D E F = L path]

V041 BLUE ABS

V042 2

V043 −

V044 BLUE X?0   [option **6** shows as **X=0?**]

V045 GTO V047   [need to block/win]

V046 GTO V077   [go to next path N]

V047 RCL D

V048 BLUE X?0   [option **1** shows as **X not =0?**]

V049 GTO V057   [D not = 0]

V050 1   [D = 0] [Note: Press 1 then ENTER]

V051 +/-   [− 1 represents the computer]

V052 BLUE STO D

V053 4   [4 because D represents cell 4]

V054 BLUE STO M

V055 YELLOW VIEW M

V056 XEQ D001   [update table, then who plays]

,,,,,,,,,,,,,,,,,,,,,

V057 RCL E

V058 BLUE X?0   [option **1** shows as **X not =0?**]

V059 GTO V067   [E not = 0]

V060 1   [E = 0] [Note: Press 1 then ENTER]

V061 +/- [− 1 represents the computer]

V062 BLUE STO E

V063 5 [5 because E represents cell 5]

V064 BLUE STO M

V065 YELLOW VIEW M

V066 XEQ D001 [update table, then who plays]

)))))))))))))))))

V067 RCL F

V068 BLUE X?0 [option **1** shows as **X not =0?**]

V069 XEQ E001 [F not = 0 GTO random choice E, Should not actually go here if program is working correctly]

Explanation for line 69: In essence, program should not go here at this stage. If it does, it means that L equaled 2 (or minus 2), but the 'missing' cell which was to be blocked was not missing.

V070 1 [F = 0] [Note: Press 1 then ENTER]

V071 +/- [− 1 represents the computer]

V072 BLUE STO F

V073 6 [6 because F represents cell 6]

V074 BLUE STO M

V075 YELLOW VIEW M

V076 XEQ D001 [update table, then who plays]

,,,,,,,,,,,,,,,,,,,,,

V077 RCL N [G H I = N path]

V078 BLUE ABS [absolute value, looking for 2 or – 2]

V079 2

V080 –

V081 BLUE X?0 [option **6** shows as **X=0?**] [will = 0 if (1 & 1) or (-1 & -1)]

V082 GTO V084 [need to block/win]

V083 GTO V115 [go to next path O]

V084 RCL G [will be 0, 1 or – 1]

V085 BLUE X?0 [option **1** shows as **X not =0?**]

V086 GTO V094 [true that G not = 0, i.e., cell 1 was already chosen]

V087 1 [therefore G = 0] [Note: Press 1 then ENTER]

V088 +/- [– 1 represents the computer]

33

V089 BLUE STO G   [stores − 1 in G]

V090 7   [7 because G represents cell 7]

V091 BLUE STO M

V092 YELLOW VIEW M

V093 XEQ D001   [update 'K tables' then to who plays]

,,,,,,,,,,,,,,,,,,,,,

V094 RCL H

V095 BLUE X?0 [option **1** shows as **X not =0?**]

V096 GTO V104 [i.e., H not = 0]

V097 1   [H = 0]   [Note: Press 1 then ENTER]

V098 +/-   [− 1 represents the computer]

V099 BLUE STO H

V100 8   [8 because H represents cell 8]

V101 BLUE STO M

V102 YELLOW VIEW M

V103 XEQ D001   [update 'K tables' then to who plays]

,,,,,,,,,,,,,,,,,,,,

V104 RCL I

V105 BLUE X?0   [option **1** shows as **X not =0?**]

V106 GTO V114 [I not = 0]

V107 1   **[I = 0]**   [Note: Press 1 then ENTER]

V108 +/-   [– 1 represents the computer]

V109 BLUE STO I

V110 9   [9 because I represents cell 9]

V111 BLUE STO M

V112 YELLOW VIEW M

V113 XEQ D001 [update 'K tables' then to who plays]

V114 XEQ E001 [random since path is finished]

Explanation for line V114: In essence, program should not go here at this stage. If it does, it means that N equaled 2 (or minus 2), but the 'missing' cell which was to be blocked was not missing.

,,,,,,,,,,,,,,,,,,,,

V115 RCL O [A D G = O path]

V116 BLUE ABS

V117 2

V118 –

V119 BLUE X?0 [option **6** shows as **X=0?**]

V120 GTO V122 [need to block/win]

V121 GTO V152 [go to next path P]

V122 RCL A

V123 BLUE X?0 [option **1** shows as **X not =0?**]

V124 GTO V132 [A not = 0]

V125 1 [A = 0] [Note: Press 1 then ENTER]

V126 +/- [− 1 represents the computer]

V127 BLUE STO A

V128 1 [1 because A represents cell 1]

V129 BLUE STO M

V130 YELLOW VIEW M

V131 XEQ D001 [update table, then who plays]

ııııııııııııııııııı

V132 RCL D

V133 BLUE X?0 [option **1** shows as **X not =0?**]

V134 GTO V142 [D not = 0]

V135 1 [D = 0] [Note: Press 1 then ENTER]

V136 +/-   [– 1 represents the computer]

V137 BLUE STO D

V138 4   [4 because D represents cell 4]

V139 BLUE STO M

V140 YELLOW VIEW M

V141 XEQ D001 [update table, then who plays]

,,,,,,,,,,,,,,,,,,,,,,,

V142 RCL G

V143 BLUE X?0 [option **1** shows as **X not =0?**]

V144 XEQ E001   [G not = 0 GTO random choice E]

Explanation for line V144: In essence, program should not go here at this stage. If it does, it means that O equaled 2 (or minus 2), but the 'missing' cell which was to be blocked was not missing.

V145 1   [G = 0] [Note: Press 1 then ENTER]

V146 +/-   [– 1 represents the computer]

V147 BLUE STO G

V148 7 [7 because G represents cell 7]

V149 BLUE STO M

V150 YELLOW VIEW M

V151 XEQ D001   [update table, then who plays]

)))))))))))))))))))

V152 RCL P [B E H = P]

V153 BLUE ABS   [absolute value, looking for 2 or – 2]

V154 2

V155 –

V156 BLUE X?0 [option **6** shows as **X=0?**]   [will = 0 if (1 & 1) or (-1 & -1)]

V157 GTO V159   [need to block/win]

V158 GTO V190   [go to next path Q]

V159 RCL B [will be 0, 1 or – 1]

V160 BLUE X?0   [option **1** shows as **X not =0?**]

V161 GTO V169 [true that B not = 0, i.e., cell 1 was already chosen]

V162 1   [therefore B = 0] [Note: Press 1 then ENTER]

V163 +/-   [– 1 represents the computer]

V164 BLUE STO B   [stores – 1 in B]

V165 2   [2 because B represents cell 2]

V166 BLUE STO M

V167 YELLOW VIEW M

V168 XEQ D001   [update 'K tables' then to who plays]

,,,,,,,,,,,,,,,,,,,,,,

V169 RCL E

V170 BLUE X?0   [option **1** shows as **X not =0?**]

V171 GTO V179   [i.e., E not = 0]

V172 1   [E = 0] [Note: Press 1 then ENTER]

V173 +/-   [− 1 represents the computer]

V174 BLUE STO E

V175 5   [5 because E represents cell 5]

V176 BLUE STO M

V177 YELLOW VIEW M

V178 XEQ D001   [update 'K tables' then to who plays]

,,,,,,,,,,,,,,,,,,,,

V179 RCL H

V180 BLUE X?0   [option **1** shows as **X not =0?**]

V181 GTO V189   [H not = 0]

V182 1   [H = 0] [Note: Press 1 then ENTER]

V183 +/-   [− 1 represents the computer]

V184 BLUE STO H

V185 8   [8 because H represents cell 8]

V186 BLUE STO M

V187 YELLOW VIEW M

V188 XEQ D001   [update 'K tables' then to who plays]

V189 XEQ E001   [random since path is finished]

Explanation for line V189: In essence, program should not go here at this stage. If it does, it means that P equaled 2 (or minus 2), but the 'missing' cell which was to be blocked was not missing.

,,,,,,,,,,,,,,,,,,,,,,,,

V190 RCL Q   [C F I = Q]

V191 BLUE ABS   [absolute value, looking for 2 or − 2]

V192 2

V193 −

V194 BLUE X?0   [option **6** shows as **X=0?**]   [will = 0 if (1 & 1) or (-1 & -1)]

V195 GTO V197 [need to block/win]

V196 GTO V228 [go to next path R]

V197 RCL C [will be 0, 1 or − 1]

V198 BLUE X?0 [option **1** shows as **X not =0?**]

V199 GTO V207 [true that C not = 0, i.e., cell 1 was already chosen]

V200 1   [therefore C = 0] [Note: Press 1 then ENTER]

V201 +/- [− 1 represents the computer]

V202 BLUE STO C [stores − 1 in C]

V203 3   [3 because C represents cell 3]

V204 BLUE STO M

V205 YELLOW VIEW M

V206 XEQ D001 [update 'K tables' then to who plays]

⁾⁾⁾⁾⁾⁾⁾⁾⁾⁾⁾⁾⁾⁾⁾⁾

V207 RCL F

V208 BLUE X?0 [option **1** shows as **X not =0?**]

V209 GTO V217 [i.e., F not = 0]

V210 1   [F = 0] [Note: Press 1 then ENTER]

V211 +/- [− 1 represents the computer]

V212 BLUE STO F

V213 6 [6 because F represents cell 6]

V214 BLUE STO M

V215 YELLOW VIEW M

V216 XEQ D001 [update 'K tables' then to who plays]

''''''''''''''''''''

V217 RCL I

V218 BLUE X?0 [option **1** shows as **X not =0?**]

V219 GTO V227 [I not = 0]

V220 1 [I = 0] [Note: Press 1 then ENTER]

V221 +/- [− 1 represents the computer]

V222 BLUE STO I

V223 9 [9 because I represents cell 9]

V224 BLUE STO M

V225 YELLOW VIEW M

V226 XEQ D001 [update 'K tables' then to who plays]

V227 XEQ E001 [random since path is finished]

Explanation for line 227: In essence, program should not go here at this stage. If it does, it means that Q equaled 2 (or minus 2), but the 'missing' cell which was to be blocked was not missing.

,,,,,,,,,,,,,,,,,,,,

V228 RCL R [A E I = R]

V229 BLUE ABS [absolute value, looking for 2 or – 2]

V230 2

V231 –

V232 BLUE X?0 [option **6** shows as **X=0?**] [will = 0 if (1 & 1) or (-1 & -1)]

V233 GTO V235 [need to block/win]

V234 GTO V266 [go to next path S]

V235 RCL A [will be 0, 1 or – 1]

V236 BLUE X?0 [option **1** shows as **X not =0?**]

V237 GTO V245 [true that A not = 0, i.e., cell 1 was already chosen]

V238 1 [therefore A = 0] [Note: Press 1 then ENTER]

V239 +/- [– 1 represents the computer]

V240 BLUE STO A [stores – 1 in A]

V241 1   [1 because A represents cell 1]

V242 BLUE STO M

V243 YELLOW VIEW M

V244 XEQ D001   [update 'K tables' then to who plays]

,,,,,,,,,,,,,,,,,,,,,,,,,,,

V245 RCL E

V246 BLUE X?0   [option **1** shows as **X not =0?**]

V247 GTO V255   [i.e., E not = 0]

V248 1   [E = 0]   [Note: Press 1 then ENTER]

V249 +/-   [− 1 represents the computer]

V250 BLUE STO E

V251 5   [5 because E represents cell 5]

V252 BLUE STO M

V253 YELLOW VIEW M

V254 XEQ D001 [update 'K tables' then to who plays]

,,,,,,,,,,,,,,,,,,,,,,,,,,,

V255 RCL I

V256 BLUE X?0   [option **1** shows as **X not =0?**]

V257 GTO V265 [I not = 0]

V258 1 [I = 0] [Note: Press 1 then ENTER]

V259 +/- [− 1 represents the computer]

V260 BLUE STO I

V261 9 [9 because I represents cell 9]

V262 BLUE STO M

V263 YELLOW VIEW M

V264 XEQ D001 [update 'K tables' then to who plays]

V265 XEQ E001 [random since path is finished]

Explanation for line 265: In essence, program should not go here at this stage. If it does, it means that R equaled 2 (or minus 2), but the 'missing' cell which was to be blocked was not missing.

,,,,,,,,,,,,,,,,,,,,,

V266 RCL S [C E G = S]

V267 BLUE ABS [absolute value, looking for 2 or − 2]

V268 2

V269 −

V270 BLUE X?0   [option **6** shows as **X=0?**]   [will = 0 if (1 & 1) or (-1 & -1)]

V271 GTO V273   [need to block/win]

V272 GTO V303   [No NEXT PATH] [Go to Random Choice]

V273 RCL C   [will be 0, 1 or − 1]

V274 BLUE X?0   [option **1** shows as **X not =0?**]

V275 GTO V283   [true that C not = 0, i.e., cell 1 was already chosen]

V276 1   [therefore C = 0] [Note: Press 1 then ENTER]

V277 +/-   [− 1 represents the computer]

V278 BLUE STO C   [stores − 1 in C]

V279 3   [3 because C represents cell 3]

V280 BLUE STO M

V281 YELLOW VIEW M

V282 XEQ D001   [update 'K tables' then to who plays]

⁄⁄⁄⁄⁄⁄⁄⁄⁄⁄⁄⁄⁄⁄⁄⁄⁄⁄

V283 RCL E

V284 BLUE X?0   [option **1** shows as **X not =0?**]

285 GTO V293   [i.e., E not = 0]

V286 1 [E = 0] [Note: Press 1 then ENTER]

V287 +/- [– 1 represents the computer]

V288 BLUE STO E

V289 5 [5 because E represents cell 5]

V290 BLUE STO M

V291 YELLOW VIEW M

V292 XEQ D001 [update 'K tables' then to who plays]

,,,,,,,,,,,,,,,,,,,,,,,

V293 RCL G

V294 BLUE X?0 [option **1** shows as **X not =0?**]

V295 GTO V303 [G not = 0]

V296 1 [G = 0] [Note: Press 1 then ENTER]

V297 +/- [– 1 represents the computer]

V298 BLUE STO G

V299 7 [7 because G represents cell 7]

V300 BLUE STO M

V301 YELLOW VIEW M

V302 XEQ D001 [update 'K tables' then to who plays]

V303 XEQ E001 [random since path is finished]

Explanation for line 303: In essence, program should not go here at this stage. If it does, it means that S equaled 2 (or minus 2), but the 'missing' cell which was to be blocked was not missing.

V304 YELLOW RTN

Press **C** to escape programming mode.

LBL V

LN = 968   Check

CK = ECAB Check

,,,,,,,,,,,,,,,,,,,,,

Program V Explanations by Statement Number:

V031 & V039 (and similar corresponding statements):

Program V checks the eight winning paths. If the path = 2 (e.g., K = 2 or -2), then two of the three variables, e.g., A, B, or C must equal either 1 or minus 1, and the remaining variable must equal 0 (i.e., the cell must be empty). However, in an abundance of caution, if the third cell was for some reason occupied, Program V will call Program E to generate a random cell choice.

As an Aside: This is an early version of the program with some built in 'safeties'. It worked well, and I was hesitant to make any changes. If one is pressed to the limit on storage, then of course, cull what is unnecessary. See also: 'As an Aside' in Appendix M.

,,,,,,,,,,,,,,,,,,,,

Program E:

Program E is the 'random move' area. A random move takes place when there is no 'pressing' need for a blocking or winning move as determined by Program V. Note that the random moves are based on the relative frequencies entered in Program B.

When relying on a repeating random process (to generate, construct, or query), one must consider if the process will eventually terminate – or can be terminated.

A VIEW, INPUT, or STOP (i.e., R/S) statement somewhere in the 'loop' will provide this termination opportunity. However, if none of these statements fit into the scheme of things, another approach must be used.

As a precaution before making a move, Program E (statements E002 to E012) checks to make sure that all nine cells are not already occupied. The cells might be occupied and play continue, for example, if the player forgets to record one of the previous moves. With this precaution, the program will print 'GAME OVER'. Otherwise, the program would search continuously for an empty cell.

Even given an empty cell, it is theoretically possible, although unlikely, that a random search for an empty cell could go on forever. Therefore, as a second precaution (statements E013 to E020), if 50 searches for an empty cell are exceeded during a given turn the program will stop and again print 'GAME OVER'.

Entering Program E:

GTO . .

BLUE PRGM

E001 BLUE LBL E

Note: See clarification below for entering the following rather tricky statement.

E002 EQN ABS(A) + ABS(B) + ABS(C) + ABS(D) + ABS(E) + ABS(F) +

ABS(G) + ABS(H) + ABS(I) > T   [Note: See number 7 below, '>' shows as solid triangle]

Entering the EQN statement:

1. Press EQN which will not be displayed.

2. BLUE ABS which will show as ABS( ) where the second parenthesis will be blinking.

3. Press RCL A witch will show as ABS(A) where the second parenthesis will still be blinking.

4. Press '>' arrow (in top right corner) to complete the above parenthesis.

5. Press +

6. Repeat the sequence BLUE ABS, RCL B, '>', then + then continue through the ninth variable.

7. After the ninth variable 'ABS(I)' press BLUE STO which will show as a solid triangular arrow, then press RCL T, you will still see a blinking cursor, then ENTER to complete the statement.

E003 RCL T

E004 9   [sum if all 9 cells are occupied]

E005 −

E006 BLUE X?0 [option **6**, will show as **X=0?**]

E007 GTO E009

E008 GTO E013

E009 YELLOW FLAGS [then **1**, then **decimal point** (will show as 1), then **0**, will show as **SF 10**, this turns off the EQN processing]

Note: Regarding the display of EQN 'Messages' see Note with Appendix F.

E010 EQN RCL G RCL A RCL M RCL E BLUE SPACE [in bottom row] RCL O RCL V RCL E RCL R ENTER [will show as **GAME OVER**]

E011 YELLOW FLAGS [then **2**, then **decimal point**, then **0**, will show as **CF 10**, this turns EQN processing back on]

E012 GTO A001

E013 0 [create a stop safety loop]

E014 BLUE STO Z

E015 1

E016 BLUE STO + Z

E017 RCL Z

E018 50 [arbitrary limit for maximum times through loop]

E019 −

E020 BLUE X?0 [option **4** shows as **X > 0?**]

E021 GTO E009 [will go here when Z = 51]

[the above statements ensure that if the unknown occurs, the program will not loop indefinitely]

E022 BLUE RAND [shows as **RANDOM**]

E023 16

E024 X

E025 YELLOW INTG [option **6** shows as **IP**]

E026 1

E027 +

E028 BLUE STO J [values 1 to 16]

E029 RCL (J) [retrieves values from 1 to 9]

E030 BLUE STO M [stores values from 1 to 9]

E031 +/-

E032 BLUE STO J [values minus 1 to minus 9]

E033 RCL (J) [0, 1, or − 1]

E034 BLUE X?0   [option **1** shows as **X not =0?**]

E035 GTO E015   [cell is occupied]

E036 RCL M   [cell was not occupied]

E037 YELLOW VIEW M   [values 1 to 9]

E038 +/-   [now M values of minus 1 to minus 9]

E039 BLUE STO J

E040 1   [press 1 the ENTER]

E041 +/-   [minus 1 represents code for the computer]

E042 BLUE STO (J)   [stores – 1 in positions minus 1 to minus 9]

E043 XEQ D001   [D updates tables]

E044 YELLOW RTN

Press **C** to escape programming mode.

LBL E

LN = 214

CK = 7396

,,,,,,,,,,,,,,,,,,,,,

Program E Explanations by Statement Number:

E002: Counts up the number of occupied cells and stores in T.

E009: Turns off the EQN processing so that the text GAME OVER can be printed.

E010: Will show **GAME OVER** if play proceeds beyond 9 moves (or computer repeatedly fails to find possible play). New game will start after pressing **R/S**.

,,,,,,,,,,,,,,,,,,,,

How to Play:

Make a little grid:

1 2 3

4 5 6

7 8 9

So that it is possible to follow along with the example, let's set the seed for the random number generator to 1279 as follows:

Type **1279 ENTER**, then **YELLOW SEED** [near the bottom right corner]

We're ready!

When you see '**W?**' enter either 0 (computer plays) or 1 (player plays).

When you see '**M?**' the player enters their move (1 to 9).

After each entry or display press **R/S** [i.e., Run/Stop]

Note: Previous moves will still be showing when you see W? and M? [Just type your new choice]

Note: After each move it will say **RUNNING** which may appear for 5 to 10 seconds.

Let's play!

XEQ A ENTER [You will see: RUNNING]

Let's let the player go first.

W? 1 R/S

M? 3 R/S

>   **M = 3 will display – press R/S**

W? 0 R/S

>   **M = 1 R/S**

W? 1 R/S

M? 5 R/S

    M = 5 R/S

W? 0

    M = 7

W? 1 R/S

M? 4 R/S

    M = 4 R/S

W? 0 R/S

    M = 6 R/S

W? 1 R/S

M? 2 R/S

    M = 2 R/S

W? 0 R/S

    M = 8 R/S

W? 1 R/S

M? 9 R/S

    M = 9

Results: In this case a draw!

Press **C** to escape

Note: If for some reason you continue to play, you will see **GAME OVER.**

Press **C** to escape.

,,,,,,,,,,,,,,,,,,,,,,

Now, we'll let the computer go first:

Type **1279 ENTER**, then **YELLOW SEED** [near the bottom right corner]

W? 0 R/S

    M = 1 R/S

W? 1 R/S

M? 5 R/S

    M = 5 R/S

W? 0

    M = 9

W? 1 R/S

M? 3 R/S

    M = 3 R/S

W? 0 R/S

  M = 7 R/S

W? 1 R/S

M? 8 R/S

  M = 8 R/S

W? 0 R/S

  M = 4 R/S [*** Win for the computer: 1,4,7 ***]

Press **C** to escape

Note: With the seed set, you may, or may not, get the same moves by the computer. It depends on the moves by the player and the resulting number of searches for a move by the computer.

,,,,,,,,,,,,,,,,,,,,,

Game's Shortcomings:

The game does have some shortcomings which could be addressed – but I'm getting old and would like to finish this book – ha ha.

With no graphics display, the player must provide the game's 'animation'.

There is no message announcing a winner. A winning path sum of 3 would indicate the player wins; a sum of -3 would indicate the computer wins.

There is not a clever exit after a win or a draw. It is necessary to press C to escape.

There is no automatic facility to alternate between turns (i.e., player and computer). One could build in a 'flip - flop'. The idea being that the answer (1 or 2) keeps being subtracted from 3. For example: $3-2 = 1$; $3-1 = 2$; $3-2 = 1$; $3-1 = 2$. See Appendix U for more details.

The previous entries still show after the W? and M?. One could clear the stack by incorporating BLUE CLEAR with option 5. See Appendix G.

The player's move is not pre-checked (the computer's move is).

There is no priority by the computer to win rather than block. To remedy this, two passes could be made through the strategy table looking first for -2 (to win), then looking for 2 (to block).

The game's response time can be a bit lengthy. Part of this is simply due to the speed of the processor, and part is due to this author's inefficient programming.

The search for a random move is inefficient and becomes even more inefficient as the game progresses. For example, let's say there are just three remaining empty cells. Rather than searching only those three cells before selecting one at random, the program searches at random even occupied cells before finding one that is empty. There is a way around this. Think of a stack with entries 1 to 9. As a cell is occupied it is placed at the bottom. Then only the remaining top 8 are searched, and this continues: the selected cell is placed at the bottom, and the top 7 are searched, etc.

,,,,,,,,,,,,,,,,,,,,

Summary:

This little book does not attempt to describe all the features of the HP 35s. A thorough description, as well as some interesting history, can be found on Wikipedia.

The book demonstrates features of the HP 35s that might be useful in game programming. It offers ideas for the tracking of moves by multiple players utilizing both offensive and defensive strategies based on 'winning paths'.

It explains the use of indices to access both direct and indirect variables, and explains the use of the EQN facility for equation processing and the display of messages and prompts.

The five programs (A, B, D, V, and E) incorporate chance and strategy considered important in most games, and demonstrate the subroutine capabilities of the HP 35s.

I hope you enjoy your HP 35s, whether you use it for fun or as a critical part of your livelihood.

,,,,,,,,,,,,,,,,,,,,

Appendix:

A. Prelims:

On and Off:

Pressing C [bottom left corner] or BLUE then C [both in bottom left corner] will turn the calculator on. YELLOW then C will turn it off.

RPN (Reverse Polish Notation):

In that we will use RPN throughout, you can switch to this mode by pressing MODE [top right] and then option 5 for RPN.

Setting the Display:

The default display is:

0.0000

0.0000

To set this display: press YELLOW then DISPLAY [top right corner], then 1 (to choose option 1FIX), then when you see 'FIX' press 4 (to choose 4 digits after the decimal point). See also Appendix E below.

Note: The Tic-Tac-Toe game resets the display to 0. (i.e., with no decimals). So after playing you may want to reset the display to the default.

,,,,,,,,,,,,,,,,,,,,

B. Program/Memory Management:

MEM Menu: Press **YELLOW MEM** and you will see [as an example]:

1VAR   2PGM

21   23,426

Option 1(VAR) will, in this case, display (using the down arrow) the values of **21** variables currently in use including the statistical registers.

Option 2 (PGM) will display the programs/labels currently in memory (see below).

The **23,426** displays, in this specific case, the currently available memory.

Checking Program Names/Labels:

To check the names (labels) of programs you have saved: Press YELLOW [bottom left] then MEM [top right corner], then 2 to select PGM (programs), then scroll up and down with the arrows [top right]. You will see something like the following:

LBL D

LN = 137

LBL A

LN = 21

LBL B

LN = 33

The first of the two lines is the program label; the second is the length of the program in bytes.

Checksum (CK =):

If you press YELLOW and then press and hold SHOW [mid left side], you will see, for example, CK = 7BA7. This is the Checksum, a unique hexadecimal number associated with this program. For example, if you delete this program and reenter the same program, you can check this Checksum to see if you have reentered it correctly. (Note: There have been reports of the Checksum not working correctly.)

Note: Even a variable name change will affect the Checksum, although a name change will not affect the program length. That is the LN = will remain the same.

Note: If you attempt to save a program with a label (LBL) already used, you will get a message: DUPLICAT.LBL

Deleting a Program:

To delete a program (after pressing YELLOW MEM option 2) simply scroll to the desired label and press BLUE CLEAR [mid right side].

See also HP 35s User's Guide 3.4, 13.22

''''''''''''''''''''''''

C. Program Editing:

To Insert a Line:

For example, you want to edit program B.

GTO B ENTER   [do this while NOT in programming mode to set the program pointer. This assumes B001, but you can also say, for example: GTO B015.]

BLUE PRGM [to switch to programming mode to display the program]

B001 LBL B

B002 INPUT X

B003 RANDOM

Maybe you want to **add** a line <u>after</u> line B002.

You will first see line B001. Scroll to line B002 (you will be adding a line <u>after</u> B002).

Start typing your new line. The pointer will immediately jump to the new line. It will say B003. Other line numbers will increment and GTO statement will adjust themselves (usually correctly).

When you are finished, simple press **C**. The new version of your program is now saved.

To Delete a Line:

Scroll to the line you want to delete and press the left facing arrow [mid right side above the CLEAR].

Note: Again the program <u>attempts</u> to adjust any GTO references for line insertions and deletions. It is, however, not always successful, and you should recheck your GTO statements.

To Edit <u>within</u> a Line:

Short commands can't really be edited. In long equations, it is sometimes possible to successfully use the left arrow [mid right side] to make certain changes. I will just say here, that I usually have better luck deleting the line I want to edit, and then simply entering the new version.

Note: From time to time when editing, you will see something ending with an underscore__. In this case it is usually necessary to press ENTER in order to continue.

Reviewing a Program:

Let's say you have entered Program F, and you would like to check that it was entered correctly:

While the 'default' numeric display is on the screen:

GTO F001 [program pointer will jump to this spot – but you will not see it jump]

BLUE PRGM [will shift to programming mode aligned and displayed at F001]

Use **^v** arrows to scroll.

Press **C** to escape programming mode. Program will automatically be saved.

Note: While the HP 35s program editor tries to adjust the GTO statements during editing (for deleted and inserted lines), it is especially important to check that this was done correctly.

See also HP 35s User's Guide 13.20

,,,,,,,,,,,,,,,,,,,,

D. Using Indexing to access the direct and indirect variables:

Four keys are important relative to accessing variables via indexing: I, (I), J and (J). Both direct and indirect variables may be accessed.

 The index variable I or J may take values from − 32 (i.e., negative 32) to 800.

− 32 through − 27 are associated with statistical registers;

− 26 through − 1 with Z through A;

0 through 800 with indirect variables.

Variables A through Z may be accessed <u>directly</u>, or <u>indirectly</u> via indexing.

Example: To store 25 in variable C using indirect access via I and (I):

− 3

STO I   [I now equals − 3]

25

STO (I)   [direct variable C now equals 25]

Example: To store 25 in indirect variable 5 using I and (I):

5

STO I   [I now equals 5]

25

STO (I) [Indirect variable 5 now equals 25]

,,,,,,,,,,,,,,,,,,,,

Note: Direct variables A through Z are identical to variables − 1 through − 26. Also keep in mind: (I) and (J) reference the same 801 indirect variables. In other words, there are <u>not</u> two sets of indirect variables.

See also HP 35s User's Guide 14.20 − 14.22

,,,,,,,,,,,,,,,,,,,,

E. DISPLAY Menu:

1FIX   2SCI

3ENG   4ALL

And further up to 10

Fixed is used in this book's examples. YELLOW DISPLAY, then select option 1, then 4 when FIX is displayed. This will display 4 digits after decimal point. Shows on the programming screen as FIX 4.

There are 10 options for things like scientific notation or to have decimal points rather than commas separating thousands, millions, etc.

See also HP 35s User's Guide 1.21

,,,,,,,,,,,,,,,,,,,,

F. FLAGS Menu:

1SF   [Set Flag]   2CF   [Clear Flag]

3FS? [Is Flag Set?]

Setting Flag 10 for example:

Press YELLOW FLAGS [Then from the menu choose option 1SF which Sets the Flags]

You will then see SF __   Press the decimal point (which enters the 1) then a zero. You will then see SF 10, which means Set Flag 10.

Note: When FLAG 10 is set, the EQN statement ignores equation processing and can therefore be used to display 'equations' as messages.

See also HP 35s User's Guide 14.9 to 14.13

,,,,,,,,,,,,,,,,,,,,

G. CLEAR Menu:

Menu Options: 1, 2, 3, 4, 5, 6

Menu will look something like the following on the screen. You must scroll to see the last line using the arrow keys in the upper right of the keypad.

1 X   2 VARS

3 ALL   4 Σ

5 STK   6 CLVARX

Option 1 Clears the X stack register.

Option 2 Clears the Direct Variable (A to Z).

Option 3 Erases EVERYTHING in memory. CLR ALL? Y N
For verification.

Option 4 Clears the 6 statistical registers.

Option 5 Clears the stack registers X Y Z T

Option 6 Clears the indirect variable registers. You will
see CLVAR___.

Usually you will enter 000 (you must type all three zeros),
which clears registers 001 to 800. Whatever number you
type, the calculator will clear (but not set to zero) all
indirect storage <u>above</u> that number.

Note: Given the above clearing procedure (i.e., clears all
numbers <u>above</u> 000), it is inconvenient to clear variable 0,
so that variable is seldom used. To clear register 0, you
must specifically store a zero in that register.

See also HP 35s User's Guide 1.5 (clearing)

,,,,,,,,,,,,,,,,,,,,

H. INTG Menu:

The INTG function is obtained by pressing the YELLOW key followed by the INTG key [middle of third row] and selecting the desired menu option. The INTG function 6 is used in essentially all of the example programs.

Menu Options: 1, 2, 3, 4, 5, 6

Menu will look something like the following on the screen. You must scroll to see the last line using the arrow keys in the upper right of the keypad.

1 SGN	2 INT[with divide sign]
3 Rmdr	4 INTG
5 FP	6 IP

Note: The characters following the option number will be displayed in the lines of your program. Although all options are shown below, only options 5 and 6 are used in the examples.

Option 1 Evaluates the number in the X register (lower screen) for the sign of the number. Will shows 1 for positive or − 1 for negative.

Option 2 Obtains the integer portion of a division. For example: 9 / 4 = 2

Explanation: With 9 in the Y register and 4 in the X register, you don't use the division key but rather the INTG function.

Option 3 Obtains the <u>remainder</u> portion of a division. For example: 9 / 4 = 1

Option 4 Calculates the greatest integer (less than or equal to).

Option 5 Obtains the fractional part of a number (i.e., to the right of the decimal).

Option 6 Obtains the integer part of a number (i.e., to the left of the decimal). It is important to note that Option 6 (which we are using) DOES NOT ROUND.

See also HP 35s User's Guide: 1.6, 4.2, C-4

,,,,,,,,,,,,,,,,,,,,

I. X?0 and the X?Y Menu:

X?0 compares the X stack register with zero.

X?Y compares the X stack register with the Y stack register.

When you press BLUE X?0 or YELLOW X?Y you will see a menu:

1 ≠ (not =)   2 ≤ (<=)   3 <

4 >   5 ≥ (>=)   6 =

To select one of the options, either enter the corresponding number, or use the arrow cursors to underline your choice and press ENTER.

We can use these features to do conditional branching. The commands are often followed by two GTO statements.

Note: The X?0 and the X?Y decision rule is: Do [next command] if true. Otherwise skip the next command.

See also HP 35s User's Guide: 14.6, 14.7, 14.8

,,,,,,,,,,,,,,,,,,,,,

J. Generating RANDOM Number Ranges:

For example, if you want random numbers from A to B:

General Formula:

Where:

A = lowest value

B = highest value

C = (B − A) + 1

D (i.e., your calculated value formula) = INTG (RAND x C) + A

Note: Remember to use option 6 with the INTG function.

Example: 5 to 10

A = 5   B = 10

C = (B − A) + 1 = 6

D = INTG(RAND x C) + A

Assume a low RAND value of 0.00123 and a high value of 0.99987

Low Value = INTG (0.00123 x 6) + 5 = 5

High Value = INTG (0.99987 x 6) + 5 = 10

Example: minus 5 to plus 5

Assume a low RAND value of 0.00123 and a high value of 0.99987

A = − 5   B = 5

C = (5 − (− 5)) + 1 = 11

D = INTG (RAND x C) + A

Low Value = INTG (0.00123 x 11) + (− 5) = − 5

High Value = INTG (0.99987 x 11) + (− 5) = 5

See also HP 35s User's Guide 4.15

,,,,,,,,,,,,,,,,,,,,,,

K. Indirect Variable Storage Requirements:

Each indirect variable requires 37 bytes of storage. Contrast this with a single programming line which requires only 3 to 4 bytes, or numbers in programs which require a varying number of bytes depending upon the number of digits. For example: 1 digit (0 − 9) = 4 bytes; 2 digit (10 − 99) = 5 bytes; 3 digit (100 − 999) = 6 bytes, etcetera. The direct storage variables A to Z are independent from, and do not subtract from, the available memory.

As an Aside: If, for some reason, you store a value in, let's say, the indirect variable location (500), upon doing this, memory is immediately also allocated for all indirect variables below that location (i.e., 0 to 499). Therefore, if you assigned location 800, i.e. the maximum limit, you will allocate essentially the total amount of memory available in the calculator. That is: 801 X 37 bytes = 29,637 bytes. Recall the total available is 30,192.

See also HP 35s User's Guide 14.20

,,,,,,,,,,,,,,,,,,,,,,

L. Comment regarding the HP 35s Subroutines:

The HP 35s has no true subroutines in the traditional sense. It does, however, have the capability to perform certain subroutine type activities such as returning to the proper spot in the calling program. Traditionally, variables in a subroutine are isolated/independent from variables with the same names in the main calling program. This is not the case with the HP 35s. However, it is specifically this lack of independence that we take advantage of in the exchange of information between the programs.

See also HP 35s User's Guide 14.1 – 14.4

,,,,,,,,,,,,,,,,,,,,,,

M. Documentation of Programs and Subroutines:

When you write a program or subroutine (because there is no capability/capacity for comments in the programs), be sure to specify in your notes: the variable names used, any variables that need to be pre-cleared, any flags that need to be set, and whether any display settings should be specified. If needed, include any instructions for playing or running, or interpretation of the output. Include the Checksum value in case you delete the program and need to reenter. (And, of course, a copy of the program is essential.)

As an Aside: I usually make a copy of my programs using Word. The HP 35s has no definitive way to escape from an infinite loop, and it is necessary to use a paperclip in the pinhole on the back side (far right) or pop the batteries (which I prefer). In either case the memory is wiped.

,,,,,,,,,,,,,,,,,,,,,,

N. Debugging Hints:

NONEXISTENT:

XEQ Z ENTER – Will say **NONEXISTENT** if there is no program Z.

XEQ Y ENTER – Will say **NONEXISTENT** if Y exists, but Y requests a subroutine or contains a GTO that does not exist. For example: You are in program Y and by mistake type (subroutine) XEQ W which does not exist, or GTO M085 which does not exist.

SYNTAX ERROR:

If you use EQN to display a message (i.e., not an actual equation to evaluate), and you forget to set FLAG 10, you will see this message.

DUPLICAT.LBL:

This means you are trying to create a program with a label that has already been used.

Stepping Through a Program:

Let's say you are having some difficulties with program 'A'. You can try the following:

GTO A001 (do this while outside programming mode, i.e., while the X/Y stack registers are showing).

Now press and hold the down arrow. You will see:

A001 LBL A

Release and repeat. You will be able to step through the program. If the program calls subroutine 'B', watch for the labels to change to 'B'. If you include extra VIEW statements at key positions in the program, this also helps. After statements like X?0, watch that the program is branching correctly.

See also HP 35s User's Guide 13.11

,,,,,,,,,,,,,,,,,,,,

O. Indirect Variables – Their Quirks and Surprises:

There are 801 indirect storage variables (000 to 800). You cannot assume they are automatically cleared or set to zero. In most cases, it is like they do not exist –they are simply not defined.

Two <u>direct</u> variables (I and J) act as the indices for, and work in conjunction with, the indirect variable functions (I) and (J). Keep in mind, there is just one indirect 'array'

(0 to 800) in spite of having two access variables (I) and (J).

Note: The variables I and J may still be used in their role as 'ordinary' direct access variables.

See also HP 35s User's Guide pages 14.20 to 14.24

As an Aside: I and J in conjunction with (I) and (J) also offer access to the <u>direct</u> access variables. For example: <u>minus</u> 1 = A, minus 2 = B . . . minus 26 = Z.

For Example:

First: Store 99 in variable A, and 88 in variable B.

Next: Run the following program:

BLUE LBL A

   − 1

BLUE STO I

YELLOW VIEW (I)   [shows A = 99, variable A is in storage position − 1]

   − 2

BLUE STO I

YELLOW VIEW (I)   [shows B = 88, variable B is in storage position – 2]

YELLOW RTN

This application offers the possibility to access the direct variables dynamically.

See also HP 35s User's Guide 14.22

,,,,,,,,,,,,,,,,,,

P. INVALID (I) or INVALID (J):

When working with indirect variables, you will frequently see the message INVALID (I) or INVALID (J).

For additional understanding of INVALID (I), do the following:

1.) BLUE CLEAR (option 6), then when you see CLVAR___ enter 000 (more about CLEAR below)

2.) Now enter 5, STO I [to set index variable I to 5]

3.) Then RCL (I)   [to recall indirect variable (5)]

You will see INVALID (I)   [essentially the indirect storage is not accessible]

Now try this:

4.) Enter 6, STO I [to set the index variable I to 6, i.e., a position higher/greater than 5]

5.) Enter 9, STO (I) [puts/stores a 9 in the indirect variable (6)]

Now let's RCL indirect variable (5):

6.) Enter 5, STO I   [sets the index variable I to 5]

7.) Then RCL (I)

You will see 0.0000 [the indirect variables lower than position (6) have been initialized to zero and are now accessible]

Note: In Step 4 above, (i.e., the 6), don't use a number higher than necessary, in that this allocates all the storage up to that number.

In step 5 above, we entered a 9. We can use any number greater than zero (zero will not work).

,,,,,,,,,,,,,,,,,,,

Q. Program D, Version 2, with VIEW Statements (in case you want to monitor the strategy values):

D001 BLUE LBL D

D002 EQN A + B + C STO K   [EQN RCL A + RCL B + RCL C BLUE STO K]

[BLUE STO will appear as a little triangle pointer]

D003 VIEW K [temporary for test]

D004 EQN D + E + F STO L

D005 VIEW L [temporary for test]

D006 EQN G + H + I STO N

D007 VIEW N [temporary for test]

D008 EQN A + D + G STO O

D009 VIEW O [temporary for test]

D010 EQN B + E + H STO P

D011 VIEW P [temporary for test]

D012 EQN C + F + I STO Q

D013 VIEW Q [temporary for test]

D014 EQN A + E + I STO R

D015 VIEW R [temporary for test]

D016 EQN C + E + G STO S

D017 VIEW S [temporary for test]

D018 GTO A006   [who plays area A INPUT W]

D019 YELLOW RTN

LBL D [with VIEW statements]

LN = 113

CK = 3732

,,,,,,,,,,,,,,,,,,,,,

R. Program Labels, Lengths, and Checksums (in hexadecimal) :

To check the length and checksums:

YELLOW, then **MEM** [top right], then option **2** (i.e., PGM), then **YELLOW**, then **SHOW** [mid left side] and hold down the SHOW key.

LBL A   LN = 62   CK = 5711

LBL B   LN = 254   CK = 0A02

LBL D   LN = 89   CK = 7FD0

LBL D   LN = 113   CK = 3232   [with VIEW statements]

LBL E   LN = 214   CK = 7396

LBL V   LN = 968   CK = ECAB

As an Aside: If you use the same program names (i.e., labels) and the same variable names, the checksums (CK =) given after the programs, should agree exactly. If different program names and variables are used, the program length (LN =) should still agree.

,,,,,,,,,,,,,,,,,,,,

S. Strategy Table for Computer's Play:

Note: Position makes no difference, only the sign and number of ones.

Cells and Path Total:

0 0 0 = 0 [no action required]

1 0 0 = 1 [no action required]

-1 0 0 = -1 [no action required]

1 -1 0 = 0 [no action required]

1 1 0 = 2 [requires action to stop player's win]

-1 -1 0 = -2 [requires action for computer to win]

1 -1 1 = 1 [no action required]

-1 1 -1 = -1 [no action required]

,,

T. Overview of the Variables Used:

The direct variables A through I are used for the nine Tic-Tac-Toe cells (accessed via the (J) indexing feature).

The direct variable J is used to index the (J) function.

The indirect variables (1 to 17) are used for the random cell selection area.

The variables W and M are used to query for 'Who' moves and the 'Move' to be made.

Variables K through S (excluding M) hold the path totals defined by Program D and queried by Program V.

Variable T is used to tally the total number of occupied cells.

,,,,,,,,,,,,,,,,,,,,,,

U. Flip - Flop:

The idea is that the answer (1 or 2) keeps being subtracted from 3.

$3 - 2 = 1$; $3 - 1 = 2$; $3 - 2 = 1$; [where 1 and 2 will indicate players' turn codes]

Z001 LBL Z [part to incorporate inside a program]

Z002 2

Z003 STO A [value of 2 gets the ball rolling]

Z004 3

Z005 STO B [stored reference value of 3]

Z006 RCL B [3]

Z007 RCL A [2 or 1]

Z008 –

Z009 STO A [1 or 2]

Z010 VIEW A [just to see what is going on]

Z011 GTO Z006

Z014 RTN

The player's turn will key on the value of A which will flip back and forth between 1 and 2.

,,,,,,,,,,,,,,,,,,,

V. HP 35s User's Guide Page References: [guide available free online]

CLEAR Menu: 1.5

Clearing Indirect Variables: 1.5

Checking and Clearing Program Labels from Memory: 1.28

Checksum: 13.23

CLVAR: 1.5

Deleting a Program: 1.28

DISPLAY: 1.21

DSE: 14.18

EQN: 13.7

FLAGS: 14.9 to 14.13

GTO: 14.4, 14.17

Indirect Variables: 14.20 to 14.24

INPUT: 13.13

Other Books by the Author:

Programming Notes and Hints for the HP 35s Scientific Calculator (2017)

Casino Games for the HP 35s Scientific Calculator – Program and Play Popular Casino Games (2020)

The Wilcoxon-Mann-Whitney Test – An Introduction to Nonparametrics – With Comments on the R Program wilcox.test (2018)

Random Numbers and the Discrete Uniform Distribution – Plus Five School Festival Games (2016) e-book only

Guide for the New Statistical Consultant – Some Suggestions and Three Key Questions to Ask (2019)

A Universal 'Pocket' Statistical Tool – Based on the Pearson Chi-Square Goodness of Fit Test (2014) e-book only

Games for School, Church, and Community Festivals: Including the Game's Statistical History (2018)

HP 35s Games and Routines for Input, Sorting, and Randomization (2020)

Postscript:

In the early '70s I saw my first electronic calculator, the Rapidman 800, a 4 function, 8 digit red LED display with fixed decimal point (2 digits to the right of the decimal). At the time it was $99, almost 20% of my monthly salary. I really needed a calculator which could do square root, which the Rapidman could not. A few 'deluxe' mechanical machines, weighing perhaps forty pounds, could churn out a square root (literally churning), but these machines were few and far between, in addition to costing a king's ransom.

The other day at a dollar store I saw a scientific calculator for – you guessed it – one dollar!

About the Author:

The author is a retired consulting statistician from The Ohio State University with degrees from The Ohio State University, Iowa State University, and Instytut Zootechniki in Krakow, Poland.